A WINNING SKILLS BOOK

You Can Handle Stress!

Joy Berry

Illustrated by Bartholomew

Joy Berry Enterprises

Copyright © Joy Berry, 2022
Originally Published 2013

All rights are reserved.

No part of this book can be duplicated or used without the prior written permission of the copyright owner, except for the use of brief quotations from the book.

For inquiries or permission requests contact the publisher.

Published by Joy Berry Enterprises
www.joyberryenterprises.com

Joy Berry
Enterprises

You can handle stress if you
- know what causes stress,
- understand how stress affects you,
- learn the four ways to deal with stress, and
- prepare yourself to deal with stress.

WHAT CAUSES STRESS

Stress is your reaction to unsettling situations. It is the way you feel and act when something disturbing happens.

An upsetting situation that causes stress is called a **stressor**. A stressor is anything that is overly unsettling.

Some stressors are positive. **Positive stressors** cause you to feel good or to benefit in some way.

WHAT CAUSES STRESS

Some stressors are negative. **Negative stressors** cause unpleasant feelings and stress that can harm you.

WHAT CAUSES STRESS

Four kinds of negative stressors can cause stress.

1. Negative Stressors Involving Your Body

Injury can cause stress.

Illness can cause stress.

2. Negative Stressors Involving Others

Conflict is disagreeing with someone. When you have a conflict with someone, you might have difficulty getting along with that person. You even might argue with him or her.

Conflict can cause stress.

Rejection is a feeling of being unwanted. It is a feeling that you are not liked or not accepted by others.

Rejection can cause stress.

Loss is what you feel when you lose something that is important to you. It is also what you experience when someone you care about
- dies,
- moves away from you, or
- leaves you and does not return.

Loss can cause stress.

3. Negative Stressors Involving Your Behavior

Misbehavior is doing something that you know is wrong. When you misbehave, you might feel guilty or afraid of getting into trouble.

Misbehavior can cause stress.

An *unfamiliar experience* is doing something that you have never done before or have not done very often.

Unfamiliar experiences can cause stress.

Failure is not succeeding at something that you try to do.

Failure can cause stress.

4. Negative Stressors Involving Your Surroundings

Uncontrollable events are events that you cannot control. Having your parents divorce and having to move are examples of uncontrollable events that can cause stress.

Unpredictable events are events that can happen without your knowing when they will begin or end. Unexpected accidents and natural disasters such as earthquakes and tornadoes are unpredictable events that can cause stress.

Other negative stressors involving your surroundings include
- irritating noises,
- extreme heat,
- extreme cold, and
- large crowds.

Here are some common stressors that young people often experience:
- Death of a family member or friend
- Death of a pet
- Having parents divorce or remarry
- Getting into trouble at home or at school
- Attending a new school
- Getting injured
- Getting sick
- Fighting with family members or friends
- Not having enough money to buy the things that are wanted or needed
- Moving to a new location
- Taking a test
- Struggling to get good grades
- Participating in an "important" competition
- Losing something that is important
- Peer pressure

HOW STRESS AFFECTS YOU

Most people react **physically** when they experience a stressor. Your body might react in one or more of these ways:
- You might breathe faster.
- Your blood pressure might increase.
- You might break out in a "cold sweat."
- Your face might turn pale.
- Your muscles might tense up.
- You might feel nauseous.

Your body's reactions to a negative stressor are called **physical stress**.

Most people also react *emotionally* when they experience a stressor. If you experience a negative stressor, you most likely will have one or more of these feelings:
- Anxiety
- Frustration
- A feeling of helplessness or being out of control
- Resentment
- Depression
- Anger

Your emotional reactions to a negative stressor are called **emotional stress**.

Your chances of suffering a great deal of physical and emotional stress are greater when you
- experience many stressors at the same time or
- experience one stressor over a very long time.

Too much physical and emotional stress can cause you to have physical problems, such as stomachaches, headaches, or backaches. Physical and emotional stress can also cause you to become sick.

HOW STRESS AFFECTS YOU

Too much physical and emotional stress can make you unhappy.

Stress can make you feel cranky and can cause you to be unfair or unkind to the people around you. This could harm your relationships with others.

Too much physical and emotional stress can be distracting. It can keep you from thinking clearly, and it can make learning difficult.

Stress can also keep you from doing what needs to be done.

Too much physical and emotional stress can lead to the development of bad habits, such as biting your nails or eating too much.

Stress can keep you from falling asleep or sleeping soundly. It can also cause you to have nightmares, or grind your teeth while you are sleeping.

FOUR WAYS TO DEAL WITH STRESS

You can learn to deal with physical and emotional stress. Depending upon the circumstances, you can
- avoid negative stressors,
- overcome negative stressors,
- adjust to negative stressors, or
- relieve the stress caused by negative stressors.

1. Avoiding Negative Stressors

If possible, avoid being around people, places, and situations that upset you. Also, try not to do things that upset you.

2. Overcoming Negative Stressors

If you can not avoid a negative stressor, you might need to overcome it. Solve the problems that negative stressors cause by following these steps:

Step One: Decide what problem needs to be solved.

Step Two: Decide what the possible solutions are.

Step Three: Consider the advantages and disadvantages that each solution offers.

Step Four: Choose the best solution.

Step Five: Do what needs to be done to solve the problem.

Step Six: Think about whether or not your actions have solved the problem in the best possible way.

3. Adjusting to Negative Stressors

If circumstances make it impossible to avoid or to overcome a negative stressor, you might need to accept it. Realize that it is part of your life. Learn to live with it.

4. Relieving the Stress Caused by Negative Stressors

You can help relieve the stress in one or more of the following ways:
- Positive self-talk
- Positive thinking
- Relaxation
- Exercise
- Emotional support
- Communication

Positive self-talk is giving yourself messages that will help you feel calm and reassured. Here are some messages to use when you experience stress:

- "I have handled problem in the past, so I know I can also handle this."
- "Things have always worked out in the past, so I know that this will work out, also."
- "Like every other problem, this problem has a solution."
- "Something good always comes out of difficult experiences. So, I know something good will come out of this experience."
- "Things are usually not as bad as they seem. So, this situation is not as bad as it seems."
- "There's a good reason for everything that happens. So I know that there is a good reason why this is happening."

Positive thinking involves clearing your mind of negative thoughts by replacing them with positive thoughts. When you need some positive thoughts to replace negative ones, think about
- a past experience that you have enjoyed,
- a future event that you are going to enjoy,
- being in a place that you truly enjoy,
- doing something that you truly enjoy,
- becoming the kind of person that you want to become, or
- being with someone you like.

Relaxation is slowing down your mind and body and encouraging them to rest.

Here is one way to relax your body: First, find a quiet place where you will not be disturbed. Lie flat on your back, stretch your legs out, place your feet slightly apart, put your arms close to your sides, turn the palms of your hands up, and close your eyes.

While you are in this position, silently count to ten. With each count, tense a part of your body, beginning with your head. By the time you reach ten your body should be completely tense from head to toe.

After you have completely tensed your body, begin again to count to ten. With each count, relax a part of your body, beginning with your toes.

Think to yourself, "My toes are completely relaxed." As you think this, relax your toes. Next, think to yourself, "My feet are completely relaxed," and relax your feet. Do the same with your legs. Then do the same thing with every part of your body. By the time you reach ten, you should be completely relaxed.

- Sometimes soothing music can enhance this process.

Exercise relieves stress by providing a positive outlet for the physical and emotional reactions that stress can cause.

Here are some examples of physical activities that can relieve stress.
- Jogging
- Dancing
- Riding a bike
- Swimming
- Doing exercises
- Playing a sport or game that requires physical effort

FOUR WAYS TO DEAL WITH STRESS

Emotional Support is comfort, reassurance, and encouragement from people who care about you. Having support from people who care about you can make you feel better when you are experiencing stress.

Communication is sharing your thoughts and feelings with other people. Communicating with others can help you feel better. It can also help you understand your problems and possibly help you to resolve them.

Because stress is a part of everyone's daily life, you need to make sure that you are prepared to deal with whatever stress comes along. This means staying healthy enough to handle stress.

Here are two ways that you can stay healthy so that you can be prepared to handle stress:

Eat healthy food. Avoid foods that contain too much
- fat,
- cholesterol,
- sugar,
- salt, and
- caffeine.

Eat the right amounts of
- fruit,
- vegetables,
- whole grains, and
- beans, nuts, seeds, poultry, fish, and other sources of protein.

Also, drink enough water to keep your body functioning properly.

Get enough rest. You need at least eight hours of sleep every day.

CONCLUSION

You might not be able to control all of the stressors in your life, but you **can** control your reactions to them. How you react determines whether or not you will be harmed by a stressor.

In other words, the effect a stressor will have on your life depends on how **you** handle it.

www.ingramcontent.com/pod-product-compliance
Lightning Source LLC
Chambersburg PA
CBHW081409070526
44583CB00020B/2734